GOLF TALES

GOLF TALES

Classic Stories from the Nineteenth Hole

WITH PHOTOGRAPHS BY MYRON BECK

INTRODUCTION BY ARNOLD PALMER

VIKING
STUDIO
BOOKS

ACKNOWLEDGMENTS

My partner Kirk Thornby and I would like to thank all those involved with this project. An especially warm thanks to Esther Mitgang and Rita Aero at Fly Productions, who were wonderful to work with. Thanks are also directed towards our staff — Kai Jorgensen and David Pelon. To Brian Toffoli, Robin Tucker, and Laurie Baer for the creativity. To David Johnston, Fred Arney, and Jill Brown for helping out.

A special thanks to the great locations and people we met while shooting the photographs in this book — to Baltusrol Golf Club and Bob Trebus, to Ralph W. Miller Golf Museum and Marge Dewey, and to the Brookside Golf Course in Pasadena.

VIKING STUDIO BOOKS
Published by the Penguin Group
Penguin Books USA Inc., 375 Hudson Street, New York, New York 10014, U.S.A.
Penguin Books Ltd, 27 Wrights Lane, London W8 5TZ, England
Penguin Books Australia Ltd, Ringwood, Victoria, Australia
Penguin Books Canada Ltd, 10 Alcorn Avenue, Toronto, Ontario, Canada M4V 3B2
Penguin Books (N.Z.) Ltd, 182–190 Wairau Road, Auckland 10, New Zealand

Penguin Books Ltd, Registered Offices:
Harmondsworth, Middlesex, England

First published in the United States of America by Viking Penguin, a division of Penguin Books USA Inc. 1991
This paperback edition published 1995

10 9 8 7 6 5 4 3 2 1

Grateful acknowledgment is made for permission to reprint the following copyrighted works:

"Golfomaniac" from *Laugh With Leacock* by Stephen B. Leacock. Copyright 1930 by Dodd, Mead & Company, renewed
    © 1958 by George Leacock. Reprinted by permission of Mrs. Barbara Nimmo.
"The Rivercliff Golf Killings" from *The Best of Don Marquis* by Don Marquis. Copyright 1921, 1928, 1929, 1930, 1934, 1935,
    1936 by Don Marquis. Reprinted by permission of Doubleday, a division of Bantam Doubleday Dell Publishing Group, Inc.
"Tee Time" by Ring Lardner, appearing in *Colliers* Magazine. Copyright 1929 by The Crowell Collier Corporation, renewed
    © 1957 by Mrs. Ring Lardner. Reprinted by permission of Ring Lardner, Jr.
"Tish Plays the Game" from *The Book of Tish* by Mary Roberts Rinehart.
    Copyright 1926 by George H. Doran Company. Reprinted by permission of Henry Holt and Company, Inc.

ISBN 0 14 02.4925 7
CIP data available.

Printed in Singapore

C O N T E N T S

ARNOLD PALMER

The game of golf was instilled into my life perhaps before I even knew it, and, to this day, it remains paramount in virtually everything I do. Why is this? Well, as I once wrote in one of my books: "Golf is deceptively simple and endlessly complicated. It satisfies the soul and frustrates the intellect. It is at the same time rewarding and maddening — and it is without a doubt the greatest game mankind has ever invented." That's how I felt then and that's how I feel now.

When I was four years old my father put a sawed-off club in my hands and showed me how to hold on to it and swing it. I can't recall a time since then when I put golf completely out of my mind. Of course, being the firstborn of a golf-course superintendent (and shortly thereafter a golf professional), whose home was right on the club grounds, had something to do with it. But I didn't *have* to like the game. Actually I didn't...I loved it!

The stories among the older members of Latrobe Country Club about "Deke's boy" are legend. How, when I was still a little kid, I used to hang around the hole beside our house because, when the ladies were playing, I knew I could collect a few nickels from them by hitting their drives over the little creek out in front of the tee. How, in my preteen years, because of the talent I was fortunate to have, my devotion to golf, and the rapid development of my game, I was able to beat the older caddies and members' sons at the club most of the time. How, when I was a teenager working

afternoons in charge of the pro shop, people would come around and find the place closed because I was somewhere out on the edge of the course hitting practice balls.

Encouraged by my father to concentrate on golf, I passed up the other high school sports that tempted me. I made the golf team as a freshman and my serious competitive career was underway. I won the Pennsylvania High School Championship twice and landed my first (of four) Western Pennsylvania Amateur Championships before I was eighteen years old. All of this helped me to get an athletic scholarship and a fine education at Wake Forest College. There I won the conference championship twice and attracted some national attention in collegiate circles. I managed to continue playing golf during most of my three-year hitch in the Coast Guard.

The direction that my adult golf career took probably surprises many people because it wasn't the typical beeline to the professional tour. The PGA Tour in the early 1950s was not the magnetic attraction for the young players that it is today. A friend in Cleveland put me in a sales position with his company that involved almost daily customer-golf, which I envisioned developing into an entire lifestyle in the mold of Bobby Jones and other gentlemen golfers of the time. That all changed when I won the National Amateur in 1954 and met Winnie Walzer. We were married before the year was out. We literally had no money, and I figured the best place to get some was on the pro tour. I had enough confidence in my

game that I was sure I could make a living as a tournament player. So I turned pro, joined the life full-time in 1955, and began the career that has been so rewarding for me and my family.

I had no idea, back in my most successful years in the early 1960s, that I would still be playing golf competitively in the 1990s. How could I or anyone else have envisioned the amazing success of the Senior PGA Tour? Instead, I was thinking about an "after-the-tour" career as a golf course designer and builder — a natural blend of my early life on the grounds of Latrobe Country Club and my playing experience. As things have turned out, I have barely slowed down my tournament schedule while moving intensively into course design. I love this business just as much as I enjoy walking off the first tee at the start of a round of golf. I never thought anything could excite me as much as playing golf. Now I have the chance to put something back into a game that has been so good to me. What great satisfaction I get when I see one of my designs turn into an exciting course — helping, I hope, to make the game as fascinating for others as it has been for me.

Obviously, the five outstanding authors whose work comprise this fine book share my fascination for the game and the humor that has always accompanied its serious side. The selection of these entertaining short stories, and the photographs by Myron Beck that illustrate them so perfectly, make *Golf Tales* a volume that will grace any golfer's library.

TEE TIME

The few devotees of golf who are not entirely unhinged realize that lessons, regular or occasional, from a competent instructor will improve their game. Even Bobby Jones, I am told, seeks advice and comfort from his old teacher when trouble with one or two clubs is making it impossible for him to get below 66 on an ordinary championship course. And the lesser lights are dissatisfied with themselves often enough to keep all our professionals busy from dawn till dark, from March till December and beyond.

Unfortunately, the trouble with the majority of golfers is not confined to one club or two but is limited only by the number of clubs they have in their bag. The average pro pays no attention to this and insists on attempting to correct your midiron faults or your driving eccentricities, to the exclusion of everything else. And more unfortunately still, the average pro fancies himself as a raconteur and when you pay ten dollars presumably for a half-hour golf lesson, what you get is a five-minute golf lesson and twenty-five minutes of funny things MacGregor and MacPherson did at St. Andrews.

In this lecture, which costs you five cents, I will try to cover as many phases of the ancient "sport" as my space allotment

RING LARDNER

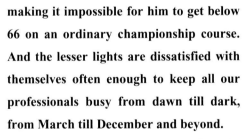

will allow, promising to lay off of any reference to twa Scotchmen till I can no longer resist. Let it be understood that I do not claim to have originated all the bits of advice and hints herein set down; some of them I have picked up from other experts and used with slight changes for the better.

As a game of golf usually begins on the first tee and as the first hole at most courses is at least a par four, I will start out with a few words about the drive. In a recent issue of *The American Golfer*, Miss Collett had an article titled "How Far Can a Woman Drive?" I could only skim it through while sorting the laundry, but the gist seemed to be that there was no limit if she would remember to stop once in a while at a filling station. I have suggested to *The American Golfer*'s editor, a southern boy, that a still more interesting article could be written not by a member of Miss Collett's sex on "How Far Can a Woman Drive a Man?" However that is apart from our topic.

The initial tee shot is made with a driver provided the people ahead of you are fifty yards or more away from the tee. If they are less than fifty yards, it is better to use a mashie or niblick and attempt to shoot over their heads instead of between them.

A mashie isn't a bad bet anyway, especially if your ball remains on the tee after you have driven. If you hit a ball with a mashie it will sometimes go farther than if you miss it with a driver.

THE ALL-IMPORTANT BALANCE

The essential of good driving is balance, and when the word balance is employed in reference to golf, it is obvious that physical balance is meant. Your weight should be evenly distributed and that often takes years because the average person with a fat stomach

usually has narrow legs and the matter of transferring part of the tonnage from one site to another can only be accomplished by studying evenings. Balance is important in other sports as well; in baseball for example. Babe Ruth has a whopping torso and ankles like a flea's. But for this uneven apportionment of weight he might develop a balance that would enable him to meet a ball squarely instead of half topping it.

Assuming that the reader is not a novice and can get off the tee in two strokes, I will take up the third shot which is generally puzzling on account of the ball being in a field of timothy or a moat or lolling against the foot of a tree.

If you haven't time to wait for the harvest or a drought or the felling of the tree, remember there is no rule forbidding the use of two clubs at once and a little practice will enable you to handle a driving iron and a putting cleek as if they were a pair of tongs. In this manner the ball may be placed in a more favorable lie or filliped onto the fairway, and from there you ought to reach the trap nearest the green with two brassies and a jigger.

Quoting again from *The American Golfer*, Chick Evans says the real shot to learn (for getting out of a trap) is the explosion shot, but "sand, because of rain and dew, has different weights, and the weight of the sand has much to do with the distance," meaning the distance you should hit behind the ball.

It is almost impossible these days to find a caddy who will carry a set of scales besides your clubs, umbrella, books, picnic lunch, spare tire, and overnight bag, but most modern locker rooms are equipped with steelyards; if yours is not, a penny or nickel weighing machine will usually be found in the nearest railroad or subway station and enough sand may be carted there in a wheelbarrow to give you an idea how much length and

strength to put into your stroke. Personally I have made a majority of my explosion shots on the fairway and with not very good results, owing, no doubt, to an unwillingness to hold up the game while the grass was being weighed.

How often we hear it said of an otherwise fine golfer that he is lamentably weak on short putts! I have never had one and so am hardly competent to instruct others how to overcome the weakness, but it seems logical to me that the player thus afflicted can get round the difficulty by not sending his approaches so near the hole.

Putting on a smooth, level green is comparatively simple and almost anybody ought to be able in three putts to get close enough so that the opponent will concede.

A different problem is presented on an uneven, rolling, tricky green, but I believe that our best golfers employ wrong methods in dealing with same. I have observed Bobby Jones, Walter Hagen and other so-called stars waste precious moments walking around, behind the ball and in front of it, to different positions from which to study the contour of the ground, thinking their eyes can be trusted to tell them how much to allow for this mound or that depression.

RESORTING TO STRATEGY

The practical way is to let the ball decide matters for itself; in other words, putt two or three times to see what happens before you go for the hole. If your first or second putt drops into the cup so much the better; if not, you at least know what the trouble was.

The golfer who finds himself in a battle with an opponent who is mechanically his superior may often win a match by the use of strategy.

For example, suppose it is your shot and the other guy's ball is ahead of yours, on the

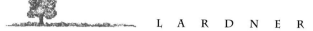 

green, in the rough, or on the fairway. You say to him, "Please move your ball," being careful to kind of mumble your words.

The instant he complies, you can claim the hole if it is a match play or have him disqualified if it is a medal play. If he attempts to defend himself by asserting he only committed the foul because you asked him to, you can pretend he misunderstood, that what you actually said was, "We move this fall."

LEGITIMATE METHODS

Three or four years ago I inadvertently got into a match with the late Walter Travis at Belleair, Fla. I was on the edge of the eighth green, about forty feet from the hole, in so many strokes. Mr. Travis was fifty yards behind me in one. "Please move your ball," he said. I did so in a spirit of levity. Mr. Travis then played a roundup shot which would have struck my ball if I hadn't moved it. As it was the ball stopped four inches from the cup. This was not an attempt at fraud on Mr. Travis' part but it gave him the match, as I picked up and went back to the clubhouse, conceding him the next eleven holes.

Another thing to remember is that while the ethics of golf forbid coughing, talking, sneezing, snoring, or making any other sort of noise while the opponent addresses the ball, it is not illegal to use mustard gas or throw flares or tickle his ears with a wisp of straw.

Mr. Alex J. Morrison (*The American Golfer* once more) writes that a man is most successful in negotiating golf shots when he is tired and therefore relaxed. It would seem, then, that a golfer facing an important match should first tire himself out. The individual probably knows best how to accomplish this in his own case. Personally I have found

the following methods almost equally effective: crawling on hands and knees from your office or home to the golf club; dancing all night with Aunt Jemima; moving the piano into the bathroom and the bathtub into the garage; arguing with a football coach.

Which reminds me of the story of the countless Scotchmen, most of them named Sandy. They were playing at St. Andrews for the first time.

"Weel," said Sandy, "gin ye swing mair hooly, Sandy, ye'll nae rax the sheugh."

"Weel," was Sandy's reply, "gin ye hae ane bittle, ye mecht misken yon clatch."

GOLFOMANIAC

We ride in and out pretty often together, he and I, on a suburban train.

That's how I came to talk to him. "Fine morning," I said as I sat down beside him yesterday and opened a newspaper.

"Great!" he answered, "the grass is drying out fast now and the greens will soon be all right to play."

"Yes," I said, "the sun is getting higher and the days are decidedly lengthening."

"For the matter of that," said my friend, "a man could begin to play at six in the morning easily. In fact, I've often wondered that there's so little golf played before breakfast. We happened to be talking about golf, a few of us last night — I don't know how it came up — and we were saying that it seems a pity that some of the best part of the day, say, from five o'clock to seven-thirty, is never used."

"That's true," I answered, and then, to shift the subject, I said, looking out of the window:

"It's a pretty bit of country just here, isn't it?"

"It is," he replied, "but it seems a shame they make no use of it — just a few market gardens and things like that. Why, I noticed along here acres and acres of just glass — some kind of houses for plants or something — and whole fields of lettuce and things like that. It's a pity

STEPHEN LEACOCK

9

they don't make something of it. I was remarking only the other day as I came along in the train with a friend of mine, that you could easily lay out an eighteen-hole course anywhere here."

"Could you?" I said.

"Oh, yes. This ground, you know, is an excellent light soil to shovel up into bunkers. You could drive some big ditches through it and make one or two deep holes — the kind they have on some of the French links. In fact, improve it to any extent."

I glanced at my morning paper. "I see," I said, "that it is again rumored that Lloyd George is at last definitely to retire."

"Funny thing about Lloyd George," answered my friend. "He never played, you know; most extraordinary thing — don't you think? — for a man in his position. Balfour, of course, was very different: I remember when I was over in Scotland last summer I had the honor of going around the course at Dumfries just after Lord Balfour. Pretty interesting experience, don't you think?"

"Were you over on business?" I asked.

"No, not exactly. I went to get a golf ball, a particular golf ball. Of course, I didn't go merely for that. I wanted to get a mashie as well. The only way, you know, to get just what you want is to go to Scotland for it."

"Did you see much of Scotland?"

"I saw it all. I was on the links at St. Andrews and I visited the Loch Lomond course and the course at Inverness. In fact, I saw everything."

"It's an interesting country, isn't it, historically?"

"It certainly is. Do you know they have played there for over five hundred years!

Think of it! They showed me at Loch Lomond the place where they said Robert the Bruce played the Red Douglas (I think that was the other party — at any rate, Bruce was one of them), and I saw where Bonnie Prince Charlie disguised himself as a caddie when the Duke of Cumberland's soldiers were looking for him. Oh, it's a wonderful country historically."

~

After that I let a silence intervene so as to get a new start. Then I looked up again from my newspaper.

"Look at this," I said, pointing to a headline, *United States Navy Ordered Again to Nicaragua*. "Looks like more trouble, doesn't it?"

"Did you see in the paper a while back," said my companion, "that the United States Navy Department is now making golf compulsory at the training school at Annapolis? That's progressive, isn't it? I suppose it will have to mean shorter cruises at sea; in fact, probably lessen the use of the navy for sea purposes. But it will raise the standard."

"I suppose so," I answered. "Did you read about this extraordinary murder case on Long Island?"

"No," he said. "I never read murder cases. They don't interest me. In fact, I think this whole continent is getting over-preoccupied with them — "

"Yes, but this case had such odd features — "

"Oh, they all have," he replied, with an air of weariness. "Each one is just boomed by the papers to make a sensation — "

"I know, but in this case it seems that the man was killed with a blow from a golf club."

"What's that? Eh, what's that? Killed him with a blow from a golf club!"

"Yes, some kind of club — "

"I wonder if it was an iron — let me see the paper — though, for the matter of that, I imagine that a blow with even a wooden driver, let alone one of the steel-handled drivers — where does it say it? — pshaw, it only just says 'a blow with a golf club.' It's a pity the papers don't write these things up with more detail, isn't it? But perhaps it will be better in the afternoon paper...."

"Have you played golf much?" I inquired. I saw it was no use to talk of anything else.

"No," answered my companion, "I am sorry to say I haven't. You see, I began late. I've only played twenty years, twenty-one if you count the year that's beginning in May. I don't know what I was doing. I wasted about half my life. In fact, it wasn't till I was well over thirty that I caught on to the game. I suppose a lot of us look back over our lives that way and realize what we have lost.

"And even as it is," he continued, "I don't get much chance to play. At the best I can only manage about four afternoons a week, though of course I get most of Saturday and all Sunday. I get my holiday in the summer, but it's only a month, and that's nothing. In the winter I manage to take a run South for a game once or twice and perhaps a little swack at it around Easter, but only a week at a time. I'm too busy — that's the plain truth of it." He sighed. "It's hard to leave the office before two," he said. "Something always turns up."

And after that he went on to tell me something of the technique of the game, illustrate it with a golf ball on the seat of the car, and the peculiar mental poise needed for driving, and the neat, quick action of the wrist (he showed me how it worked) that is needed to

undercut a ball so that it flies straight up in the air. He explained to me how you can do practically anything with a golf ball, provided that you keep your mind absolutely poised and your eye in shape, and your body a trained machine. It appears that even Bobby Jones of Atlanta and people like that fall short very often from the high standard set up by my golfing friend in the suburban car.

So, later in the day, meeting someone in my club who was a person of authority on such things, I made inquiry about my friend. "I rode into town with Llewellyn Smith," I said. "I think he belongs to your golf club. He's a great player, isn't he?"

"A great player!" laughed the expert. "Llewellyn Smith? Why, he can hardly hit a ball! And anyway, he's only played about twenty years!"

THE RIVERCLIFF GOLF KILLINGS

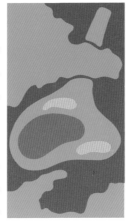

I am telling this story to the public just as I told it in the grand jury room; the district attorney having given me a carbon copy of my sworn testimony.

THE CASE OF DOC GREEN

QUESTION: Professor Waddems, when did you first notice that Dr. Green seemed to harbor animosity towards you?

ANSWER: It was when we got to the second hole.

QUESTION: Professor, you may go ahead and tell the jury about it in your own words.

ANSWER: Yes, sir. The situation was this: My third shot lay in the sand in the shallow bunker — an easy pitch with a niblick to within a foot or two of the pin, for anyone who understands the theory of niblick play as well as I do. I had the hole in five, practically.

"Professor," said Doc Green, with whom I was playing —

QUESTION: This was Dr. James T. Green, the eminent surgeon, was it not?

ANSWER: Yes, sir. Dr. Green, with whom I was playing, remarked, "You are all wrong about Freud. Psychoanalysis is the greatest discovery of the age."

"Nonsense! Nonsense! Nonsense!" I replied. "Don't be a fool, Doc! I'll show you where Freud is all wrong, in a minute."

DON MARQUIS

15

And I lifted the ball with an explosion shot to a spot eighteen inches from the pin, and holed out with an easy putt.

"Five," I said and marked it on my card.

"You mean eight," said Doc Green.

"Three into the bunker, four onto the green, and one putt — five," I said.

"You took four strokes in the bunker, Professor," he said. "Every time you said 'Nonsense' you made a swipe at the ball with your niblick."

"Great Godfrey," I said, "you don't mean to say you are going to count those gestures I made to illustrate my argument as *golf strokes*? Just mere gestures! And you know very well I have never delivered a lecture in twenty-five years without gestures like that!"

"You moved your ball an inch or two with your club at every gesture," he said.

QUESTION: Had you really done so, Professor? Remember, you are on oath.

ANSWER: I do not remember. In any case, the point is immaterial. They were merely gestures.

QUESTION: Did you take an eight, or insist on a five?

ANSWER: I took an eight. I gave in. Gentlemen, I am a good-natured person. Too good-natured. Calm and philosophical; unruffled and patient. My philosophy never leaves me. I took an eight.

(*Sensation in the grand jury room.*)

QUESTION: Will you tell something of your past life, Professor Waddems — who you are and what your lifework has been, and how you acquired the calmness you speak of?

ANSWER: For nearly twenty-five years I lectured on philosophy and psychology in

various universities. Since I retired and took up golf it has been my habit to look at all the events and tendencies in the world's news from the standpoint of the philosopher.

QUESTION: Has this helped you in your golf?

ANSWER: Yes, sir. My philosophical and logical training and my specialization in psychology, combined with my natural calmness and patience, have made me the great golfer that I really am.

QUESTION: Have you ever received a square deal, Professor, throughout any eighteen holes of golf?

ANSWER: No, sir. Not once! Not once during the five years since I took the game up at the Rivercliff Country Club.

QUESTION: Have you ever broken a hundred, Professor Waddems?

ANSWER: No, sir. I would have, again and again, except that my opponents, and other persons playing matches on the course, and the very forces of nature themselves are always against me at critical moments. Even the bullfrogs at the three water holes treat me impertinently.

QUESTION: Bullfrogs? You said the bullfrogs, Professor?

ANSWER: Yes, sir. They have been trained by the caddies to treat me impertinently.

QUESTION: What sort of treatment have you received in the locker room?

ANSWER: The worst possible. In the case under consideration, I may say that I took an eight on the second hole, instead of insisting on a five, because I knew the sort of thing Dr. Green would say in the locker room after the match — I knew the scene he would make, and what the comments of my so-called friends would be. Whenever I do get down to a hundred an attempt is made to discredit me in the locker room.

QUESTION: Well, you took an eight on the second hole. What happened at the third hole?

ANSWER: Well, sir, I teed up for my drive, and just as I did so, Doc Green made a slighting remark about the League of Nations. "I think it is a good thing we kept out of it," he said.

QUESTION: What were your reactions?

ANSWER: A person of intelligence could only have one kind of reaction, sir. The remark was silly, narrow-minded, provincial, boneheaded, crass, and ignorant. It was all the more criminal because Dr. Green knew quite well what I think of the League of Nations. The League of Nations was my idea. I thought about it even before the late President Wilson did, and talked about it and wrote about it and lectured about it in the university.

QUESTION: So that you consider Dr. Green's motives in mentioning it when you were about to drive —

ANSWER: The worst possible, sir. They could only come from a black heart at such a time.

QUESTION: Did you lose your temper, Professor?

ANSWER: No, sir! No, sir! No, sir! I *never* lose my temper! Not on any provocation. I said to myself, Be calm! Be philosophical! He's trying to get me excited! Remember what he'll say in the locker room afterwards! Be calm! Show him, show him, show him! Show him he can't get my goat.

QUESTION: Then you drove?

ANSWER: I addressed the ball the second time, sir. And I was about to drive when he

said, with a sneer, "You must excuse me, Professor. I forgot that you invented the League of Nations."

QUESTION: Did you become violent, then, Professor?

ANSWER: No, sir! No, sir! I never become violent! I never —

QUESTION: Can you moderate your voice somewhat, Professor?

ANSWER: Yes, sir. I was explaining that I never become violent. I had every right to become violent. Any person less calm and philosophical would have become violent. Doc Green to criticize the League of Nations! The ass! Absurd! Preposterous! Silly! Abhorrent! Criminal! What the world wants is peace! Philosophic calm! The fool! Couldn't he understand that!

QUESTION: Aren't you departing, Professor, from the events of the 29th of last September at the Rivercliff golf course? What did you do next?

ANSWER: I drove.

QUESTION: Successfully?

ANSWER: It was a good drive, but the wind caught it, and it went out of bounds.

QUESTION: What did Dr. Green do then?

ANSWER: He grinned. A crass bonehead capable of sneering at the progress of the human race would sneer at a time like that.

QUESTION: But you kept your temper?

ANSWER: All my years of training as a philosopher came to my aid.

QUESTION: Go on, Professor.

ANSWER: I took my midiron from my bag and looked at it.

QUESTION: Well, go on, Professor. What did you think when you looked at it?

20

ANSWER: I do not remember, sir.

QUESTION: Come, come, Professor! You are under oath, you know. Did you think what a dent it would make in his skull?

ANSWER: Yes, sir. I remember now. I remember wondering if it would not do his brain good to be shaken up a little.

QUESTION: Did you strike him, then?

ANSWER: No, sir. I knew what they'd say in the locker room. They'd say that I lost my temper over a mere game. They would not understand that I had been jarring up his brain for his own good, in the hope of making him understand about the League of Nations. They'd say I was irritated. I know the things people always say.

QUESTION: Was there no other motive for not hitting him?

ANSWER: I don't remember.

QUESTION: Professor Waddems, again I call your attention to the fact that you are under oath. What was your other motive?

ANSWER: Oh yes, now I recall it. I reflected that if I hit him they might make me add another stroke to my score. People are always getting up the flimsiest excuses to make me add another stroke. And then accusing me of impatience if I do not acquiesce in their unfairness. I am never impatient or irritable!

QUESTION: Did you ever break a club on the course, Professor?

ANSWER: I don't remember.

QUESTION: Did you not break a mashie on the Rivercliff course last week, Professor Waddems? Reflect before you answer.

ANSWER: I either gave it away or broke it, I don't remember which.

QUESTION: Come, come, don't you remember that you broke it against a tree?

ANSWER: Oh, I think I know what you mean. But it was not through temper or irritation.

QUESTION: Tell the jury about it.

ANSWER: Well, gentlemen, I had a mashie that had a loose head on it, and I don't know how it got into my bag. My ball lay behind a sapling, and I tried to play it out from behind the tree and missed it entirely. And then I noticed I had this old mashie, which should have been gotten rid of long ago. The club had never been any good. The blade was laid back at the wrong angle. I decided that the time had come to get rid of it once and for all. So I hit it a little tap against the tree, and the head fell off. I threw the pieces over into the bushes.

QUESTION: Did you swear, Professor?

ANSWER: I don't remember. But the injustice of this incident was that my opponent insisted on counting it as a stroke and adding it to my score — my judicial, deliberate destruction of this old mashie. I never get a square deal.

QUESTION: Return to Dr. James T. Green, Professor. You are now at the third hole, and the wind has just carried your ball out of bounds.

ANSWER: Well, I didn't hit him when he sneered. I carried the ball within bounds.

"Shooting three," I said calmly. I topped the ball. Gentlemen, I have seen Walter Hagen top the ball the same way.

"Too bad, Professor," said Doc Green. He said it hypocritically. I knew it was hypocrisy. He was secretly gratified that I had topped the ball. He knew I knew it.

QUESTION: What were your emotions at this further insult, Professor?

ANSWER: I pitied him. I thought how inferior he was to me intellectually, and I pitied him. I addressed the ball again. "I pity him," I murmured. "Pity, pity, pity, pity, pity!"

He overheard me. "Your pity has cost you five more strokes," he said.

"I was merely gesticulating," I said.

QUESTION: Did the ball move? Remember, you are under oath, and you have waived immunity.

ANSWER: If the ball moved, it was because a strong breeze had sprung up.

QUESTION: Go on.

ANSWER: I laid the ball upon the green and again holed out with one putt. "I'm taking a five," I said, marking it on my card.

"I'm giving you a ten," he said, marking it on his card. "Five gesticulations on account of your pity."

QUESTION: Describe your reactions to this terrible injustice, Professor. Was there a red mist before your eyes? Did you turn giddy and wake up to find him lying lifeless at your feet? Just what happened?

ANSWER: Nothing, sir.

(*Sensation in the grand jury room.*)

QUESTION: Think again, Professor. Nothing?

24

ANSWER: I merely reflected that, in spite of his standing scientifically, Dr. James T. Green was a moron and utterly devoid of morality and that I should take this into account. I did not lose my temper.

QUESTION: Did you snatch the card from his hands?

ANSWER: I took it, sir. I did not snatch it.

QUESTION: And then did you cram it down his throat?

ANSWER: I suggested that he eat it, sir, as it contained a falsehood in black and white, and Dr. Green complied with my request.

QUESTION: Did you lay hands upon him, Professor? Remember, now, we are still talking about the third hole.

ANSWER: I think I did steady him a little by holding him about the neck and throat while he masticated and swallowed the card.

QUESTION: And then what?

ANSWER: Well, gentlemen, after that there is very little more to tell until we reached the sixteenth hole. Dr. Green for some time made no further attempt to treat me unjustly and played in silence, acquiescing in the scores I had marked on my card. We were even as to holes, and it was a certainty that I was about to break a hundred. But I knew what was beneath this silence on Doc Green's part, and I did not trust it.

QUESTION: What do you mean? That you knew what he was thinking, although he did not speak?

ANSWER: Yes, sir. I knew just what kind of remarks he would have made if he had made any remarks.

QUESTION: Were these remarks which he suppressed derogatory remarks?

ANSWER: Yes, sir. Almost unbelievably so. They were deliberately intended to destroy my poise.

QUESTION: Did they do so, Professor?

ANSWER: I don't think so.

QUESTION: Go on, Professor.

ANSWER: At the sixteenth tee, as I drove off, this form of insult reached its climax. He accentuated his silence with a peculiar look, just as my club head was about to meet the ball. I knew what he meant. He knew that I knew it, and that I knew. I sliced into a bunker. He stood and watched me, as I stepped into the sand with my niblick — watched me with that look upon his face. I made three strokes at the ball and, as will sometimes happen even to the best of players, did not move it a foot. The fourth stroke drove it out of sight into the sand. The sixth stroke brought it to light again. Gentlemen, I did not lose my temper. I never do. But I admit that I did increase my tempo. I struck rapidly three more times at the ball. And all the time Doc Green was regarding me with that look, to which he now added a smile. Still I kept my temper, and he might be alive today if he had not spoken.

QUESTION (*by the foreman of the jury*): What did the man say at this trying time?

ANSWER: I know that you will not believe it is within the human heart to make the black remark that he made. And I hesitate to repeat it. But I have sworn to tell everything. What he said was, "Well, Professor, the club puts these bunkers here, and I suppose they have got to be used."

QUESTION (*by the foreman of the jury*): Was there something especially trying in the way he said it?

ANSWER: There was. He said it with an affectation of joviality.

QUESTION: You mean as if he thought he were making a joke, Professor?

ANSWER: Yes, sir.

QUESTION: What were your emotions at this point?

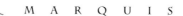

ANSWER: Well, sir, it came to me suddenly that I owed a duty to society; and for the sake of civilization I struck him with the niblick. It was an effort to reform him, gentlemen.

QUESTION: Why did you cover him with sand afterwards?

ANSWER: Well, I knew that if the crowd around the locker room discovered that I had hit him, they would insist on counting it as another stroke. And that is exactly what happened when the body was discovered — once again I was prevented from breaking a hundred.

THE DISTRICT ATTORNEY: Gentlemen of the jury, you have heard Professor Waddems' frank and open testimony in the case of Dr. James T. Green. My own recommendation is that he be not only released, but complimented, as far as this count is returned. If ever a homicide was justifiable, this one was. And I suggest that you report no indictment against the Professor, without leaving your seats. Many of you will wish to get in at least nine holes before dinner. Tomorrow Professor Waddems will tell us what he knows about the case of Silas W. Amherst, the banker.

⌒

The district attorney has given me the following certified copy of my sworn testimony, and I am telling the story of this golf game to the public just as I told it in the grand jury room.

THE CASE OF SILAS W. AMHERST, BANKER

QUESTION: Professor Waddems, will you tell the jury just when it was that you first noted evidences of the criminal tendencies, amounting to total depravity, in the late Silas W. Amherst?

ANSWER: It was on the 30th of September, 1936, at 4:17 p.m.

QUESTION: Where were you when you first began to suspect that the man had such an evil nature?

ANSWER: On the Rivercliff golf course, sir, at the second hole.

QUESTION: A par-four hole, Professor?

ANSWER: It is called that, yes, sir; but it is unfairly trapped.

QUESTION: What is your usual score on this hole, Professor Waddems? Remember, you are on oath, and you have waived immunity in this inquiry.

ANSWER: I have never yet received fair treatment with regard to this hole. My normal score on this hole is five, with an occasional par four and sometimes a birdie three. But disgraceful tactics have always been employed against me on this hole to prevent me from playing my normal game.

QUESTION: Is it a water hole?

ANSWER: Yes, sir.

QUESTION: Is it the same water hole from which the body of Silas W. Amherst was removed on October 3, 1936, a few days after he was last seen alone with you?

ANSWER: No, sir. That was the fifteenth hole. The water at the fifteenth hole is much deeper than the water at the second hole or the seventh hole. In the water at the fifteenth hole there are now several other bod —

QUESTION: Be careful, Professor! This inquiry is devoted entirely to Silas W. Amherst, and you are not compelled to incriminate or degrade yourself. Professor, are you a nervous, irritable, testy, violent person?

ANSWER: No, sir! No, sir! No, sir! And the man that dares to call me that is...

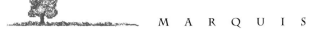 
(*A portion of Prof. Waddems' reply is stricken from the record.*)

QUESTION: Quietly, Professor, quietly! Tell these gentlemen how you gained the unruffled patience and philosophic calm that have made you the great golfer that you are.

ANSWER: For twenty-five years I lectured on philosophy and psychology at various universities. And I apply these principles to my golf game.

QUESTION: In spite of your thorough scientific knowledge of the game, have you ever broken a hundred?

ANSWER: Yes, sir; yes, sir; yes, sir!

QUESTION: Mildly, please, Professor! Quietly! I will put the question in a different way. Professor, has any opponent with whom you played ever *admitted* that you broke a hundred, or has any card that you turned in after playing around alone been credited, if it showed you *had* broken a hundred?

ANSWER: I don't remember, sir. My game has been misrepresented and persecuted for years at Rivercliff.

QUESTION: To return to Mr. Amherst. Tell the jury exactly what happened at the second hole which revealed the man's irreclaimable blackness of character.

ANSWER: Well, sir, I teed up for my drive and addressed the ball. And just as I brought my club back, and it was poised for the down stroke, he said to me:

"Professor, you're driving with a brassie, aren't you?"

I gave him a look of mild expostulation, checked the drive, and stood in front of the ball again.

"I don't think your stance is right, Professor," he said. "Let me show you the proper

31

stance — you don't mind my showing you, do you, Professor?"

Then he proceeded to show me — and I may say in passing that his theories were entirely faulty.

"I noticed on the first tee," he went on, "that you didn't understand how to pivot. You want to get your body into it, Professor. Like this," and he made a swing in demonstration.

"Your instruction, Mr. Amherst," I said politely, "is entirely gratuitous and all wrong."

"I thought you'd be glad to have me show you, Professor," he said. "And if I were you, I wouldn't play that new ball on this water hole. Here, I'll lend you a floater."

And the man actually took from his bag a floater, removed my ball, and teed up the one he had lent me.

"Now, Professor," he said, "a little more freedom in your swing. Keep your eye on the ball and don't let your hands come through ahead of the club. I noticed you had a tendency that way. I think your grip is wrong, Professor. Oh yes, certainly wrong! Here, let me show you the correct grip. And keep your head down, keep your head down!"

QUESTION: Was it then, Professor, that the tragedy occurred?

ANSWER: No, sir! No, sir! No, sir!

QUESTION: Quietly, Professor, quietly! You remained calm?

32

ANSWER: I am always calm! I never lose my temper! I am always patient! Self-contained! Restrained! Philosophical! Unperturbed! Nothing excites me! Nothing, I say, nothing! Nothing! Nothing! Nothing!

QUESTION: There, there, Professor, easily, easily now! What happened next?

ANSWER: I took a driving iron from my bag and addressed the ball again. I —

QUESTION: Just a moment, Professor. Why did you not continue with the brassie?

ANSWER: It was broken, sir.

QUESTION: Broken? How? I do not understand. How did it become broken?

ANSWER: I do not remember.

QUESTION: Between Mr. Amherst's instruction with the brassie and your taking the driving iron from the bag, as I understand it, the brassie was somehow broken. Please fill up this interval for the jury. What happened?

ANSWER: I can't recall, sir.

QUESTION: Come, come, Professor! How was the brassie broken?

ANSWER: It hit the sandbox, sir.

QUESTION: How could it hit the sandbox?

ANSWER: Well, it was an old brassie, and after I had made a few practice swings with it, I decided that it was poorly balanced and that I had better get rid of it once and for all. I did not wish to give it to a caddie, for I do not think it is fair to give poor clubs to these boys who are earnestly striving to educate themselves to be professionals; they are poor boys, for the most part, and we who are in better circumstances should see that they have a fair start in life. So I broke the brassie against the sandbox and took my driving iron, and —

QUESTION: Just a minute, Professor! These practice strokes that you made with the brassie, were there five or six of them?

ANSWER: I don't recollect, sir.

QUESTION: Did any one of them hit the ball?

ANSWER: No, sir! No, sir! No, sir! The brassie never touched the ball! The ball moved because there was a bent twig under it — this man Amherst had teed up his floater for me with a pat of sand upon a bent twig — and the twig straightened up and moved the sand, and the ball rolled off of it.

QUESTION (*by the foreman of the jury*): Professor Waddems, how far did the ball roll when the twig straightened up?

ANSWER: Well, sir, it had been teed up at the very edge of the driving green, and the ground is pretty high there, and the ball rolled down the slope, and it gained a great deal of momentum as it rolled down the slope, like an avalanche as it comes rolling down a mountainside, and at the bottom of the slope it struck a rut in the road the work-and-upkeep wagons use on the course, and that rut connects with the asphalt drive that leads in to the clubhouse, and when the ball struck the asphalt road it had already gained so much momentum that it rolled for some distance along the asphalt road, and then it crashed into the underbrush near the road and hit a sapling and bounded over onto the first fairway, all on account of the slope of the ground, for it had never been touched with the brassie at all.

QUESTION: Professor, did this happen to the ball five or six times before you discarded the brassie and took the driving iron?

ANSWER: No, sir. I only recall three times.

QUESTION: Go on, Professor. After these practice strokes, and your breaking of the brassie, you took the driving iron. What happened then?

ANSWER: Then Mr. Amherst stepped up and said to me, "Professor, let me give you a few tips about iron play. And you must keep your head down, keep your head down!"

35

QUESTION: Did you lose your temper then?

ANSWER: I never lose my temper! Never! Never! Never!

QUESTION: Quietly, now, Professor, quietly! Go on.

ANSWER: I made a magnificent drive, which cleared the water jump, and my second shot was on the green. I holed out with two putts. "A par four," I said, marking it on my card.

"You mean nine," said this man Amherst. Gentlemen, he had the effrontery to claim that the five practice swings I had made with the brassie, just simply to humor him in his demonstrations, were actual golf strokes!

(*Sensation in the grand jury room. Cries of "Outrageous!" "Impossible!" "The Dastard!" from various grand jurymen. The outburst quelled with difficulty by the district attorney.*)

QUESTION (*by the foreman of the jury*): Professor Waddems, did you end it all then?

ANSWER: No, sir. I kept my self-control. Gentlemen, I am always for peace! I am a meek person. I am mild. I will endure persecution to a point beyond anything that is possible to a man who has not had my years of training in philosophy and applied psychology. I merely got another caddie and proceeded with the game, yielding the point to Mr. Amherst for the sake of peace.

QUESTION: Got another caddie?

ANSWER: Yes, sir. The one I started out with was injured.

QUESTION: How, Professor?

ANSWER: I don't remember.

QUESTION: Think, Professor! Was it by a fall?

ANSWER: Oh yes, now I recollect! It *was* by a fall. The caddie fell from a tree just beyond the second green and broke his shoulder.

QUESTION: What was he doing in the tree?

ANSWER: He had retired to the top of the tree under a peculiar misapprehension, sir. He had agreed with Mr. Amherst with regard to the question as to whether I should take nine strokes or a par four; and I think he misinterpreted some sudden motion of mine as a threat.

QUESTION: A motion with a golf club?

ANSWER: It may have been, sir. I had a club in my hand, and I remember that my mind at the moment was engrossed with a problem connected with the underlying psychology of the full swing with wooden clubs.

QUESTION: Well, Professor, the caddie is now at the top of the tree, laboring under a misapprehension. What caused his fall?

ANSWER: I think the wooden club must have slipped somehow from my hands, sir. It flew to the top of the tree and disturbed his balance, causing him to fall.

QUESTION: Was he a good caddie?

ANSWER: There are no good caddies, sir.

(Ripple of acquiescent laughter goes round the grand jury room.)

QUESTION: Then, Professor, you went on to the next driving green. Tell what happened from this point on to the fifteenth hole, where the body of Silas W. Amherst was found four days later.

ANSWER: Advice, sir, advice! That's what happened! Advice! One long, intolerable gehenna of gratuitous advice! Gentlemen, I don't know whether any of you ever had the misfortune to play golf with the late Silas W. Amherst, but if you had —

(*Cries from various grand jurors: "Yes, yes, I played with him!" "Ataboy, Professor!" "I knew him, Prof!" etc., etc. District attorney begs for order; witness continues.*)

ANSWER: Advice! Advice! Advice! And always the fiendish malignity of the man concealed under a cloak of helpful friendliness! Advice! Advice! Advice! And to me! I, who have studied the basic principles of the game more thoroughly than any other man in America today! Gentlemen, if I were not the most patient man in the world, Silas W. Amherst would have bit the dust twenty times between the second and the fifteenth holes that day! His explanations — to me! His continual babble and chatter! His demonstrations! Every club I took from my bag, he *explained* to me! Gentlemen, some of them were clubs that I had designed myself and had had manufactured to fit my own original theories with regard to golf! But I kept my temper! I never lose my temper! Never! Never! Never!

QUESTION: Does any particularly insulting phrase of advice stand out in your memory, Professor?

ANSWER: Yes, sir! A dozen times on every hole he would cry to me as I addressed the ball, "Keep your head down, Professor, keep your head down!"

THE DISTRICT ATTORNEY: Please sit down, Professor; and do not bang on the chairs with your walking stick as you talk. We cannot hear your testimony.

THE PROFESSOR: Yes, sir. Well, at the fifteenth hole, while he was standing on the edge of the water, looking for a ball —

QUESTION: Professor, is it true that the fifteenth hole at Rivercliff is really a pool, fed by subterranean springs, and so deep that no plummet has ever sounded its bottom?

39

ANSWER: Exactly, sir. As Silas W. Amherst stood on the edge of it, it occurred to me that perhaps the man's conscience had awakened and that he was going to commit suicide for the good of the human race, gentlemen. And so I gave him a little pat of approval — on the back; and he fell in. Gentlemen, he judged himself and executed himself, and I still approve.

QUESTION: Would you mind telling the jurors, Professor, just what Mr. Amherst said immediately before you patted him approvingly on the back?

ANSWER: He said, "You just stick to me, Professor, and do as I show you, and I'll make some kind of golfer out of you yet."

QUESTION: Did he try to struggle to land, and did you hold his head under water?

ANSWER: Yes, sir, I generously assisted him in his purpose to that extent.

QUESTION: What did you say while you were assisting him?

ANSWER: I said, "Keep your head down, Mr. Amherst, keep your head down!"

THE FOREMAN OF THE JURY: Mr. District Attorney, speaking for the other members of this jury as well as for myself, it is ridiculous to consider the matter of finding any true bill of indictment of any sort against Professor Waddems in the case of the late Mr. Amherst. The pat of approval was more than justified, and we consider Professor Waddems a public benefactor.

THE DISTRICT ATTORNEY: Tomorrow we will take up the case of Willie, alias "Freckled," Briggs, the caddie who met his death on October 4, 1936, at the Rivercliff Country Club. I suggest that the slight rain we have had today, which is happily over with, should contribute greatly to what is known as a good brassie lie on the fairways. You are dismissed for the day.

Tish Plays the Game

We met Nettie Lynn on the street the other day, and she cut us all dead. Considering the sacrifices we had all made for her, especially our dear Tish, who cut a hole in her best rug on her account, this ungrateful conduct forces me to an explanation of certain events which have caused most unfair criticism. Whatever the results, it is never possible to impugn the motives behind Tish's actions.

As for the janitor of Tish's apartment house maintaining that the fruit jar buried in the floor was a portion of a still for manufacturing spirituous liquors, and making the statement that Tish's famous blackberry cordial for medicinal use was fifty percent alcohol — I consider this beneath comment. The recipe from which this cordial is made was originated by Tish's Great-aunt Priscilla, a painting of whom hangs, or rather did hang, over the mantel in Tish's living room.

The first notice Aggie and I received that Tish was embarked on one of her kindly crusades again was during a call from Charlie Sands. We had closed our cottage at Lake Penzance and Aggie was spending the winter with me. She had originally planned to go to Tish, but at the last moment Tish had changed her mind.

MARY ROBERTS RINEHART

"You'd better go with Lizzie, Aggie," she said. "I don't always want to talk, and you do."

As Aggie had lost her upper teeth during an unfortunate incident at the lake, which I shall relate further on, and as my house was near her dentist's, she agreed without demur. To all seeming the indications were for a quiet winter, and save for an occasional stiffness in the arms, which Tish laid to neuritis, she seemed about as usual.

In October, however, Aggie and I received a visit from her nephew, and after we had given him some of the cordial and a plate of Aggie's nut wafers he said, "Well, revered and sainted aunts, what is the old girl up to now?"

We are not his aunts, but he so designates us. I regret to say that by "the old girl" he referred to his Aunt Letitia.

"Since the war," I said with dignity, "your Aunt Letitia has greatly changed, Charlie. We have both noticed it. The great drama is over, and she is now content to live on her memories."

I regret to say that he here exclaimed, "Like ——— she is! I'll bet you a dollar and a quarter she's up to something right now."

Aggie gave a little moan.

"You have no basis for such a statement," I said sternly. But he only took another wafer and more of our cordial. He was preventing a cold.

"All right," he said. "But I've had considerable experience, and she's too quiet. Besides, she asked me the other day if doubtful methods were justifiable to attain a righteous end!"

"What did you tell her?" Aggie inquired anxiously.

"I said they were not; but she didn't seem to believe me. Now mark my words: After every spell of quiet she has she goes out and gets in the papers. So don't say I haven't warned you."

But he had no real basis for his unjust suspicions, and after eating all the nut wafers in the house he went away.

"Just one thing," he said: "I was around there yesterday, and her place looked queer to me. I missed a lot of little things she used to have. You don't suppose she's selling them, do you?"

Well, Tish has plenty of money and that seemed unlikely. But Aggie and I went around that evening, and it was certainly true. Her Cousin Mary Evans' blue vases were gone from the mantel of the living room, and her Great-aunt Priscilla's portrait was missing from over the fireplace. The china clock with wild roses on it that Aggie had painted herself had disappeared, and Tish herself had another attack of neuritis and had her right arm hung in a sling.

She was very noncommital when I commented on the bareness of the room.

"I'm sick of being cluttered up with truck," she said. "We surround our bodies with too many things, and cramp them. The human body is divine and beautiful, but we surround it with — er — china clocks and what not, and it deteriorates."

"Surround it with clothes, Tish," I suggested, but she waved me off.

"Mens sana in corpore sano," she said.

She had wrenched her left knee, too, it appeared, and so Hannah let us out. She went into the outside corridor with us and closed the door behind her.

"What did she say about her right arm and her left leg?" she inquired.

When we told her she merely sniffed.

"I'll bet she said she was sick of her aunt's picture and that clock, too," she said. "Well, she's lying, that's all."

"Hannah!"

"I call it that. She's smashed them, and she's smashed her Grandfather Benton and the cut-glass salad bowl, and a window. And the folks below are talking something awful."

"Hannah! What do you mean?"

"I don't know," Hannah wailed, and burst into tears. "The things she says when she's locked me out! And the noise! You'd think she was killing a rat with the poker. There's welts an inch deep in the furniture, and part of the cornice is smashed. Neuritis! She's lamed herself, that's all."

"Maybe it's a form of physical culture, Hannah," I suggested. "They jump about in that, you know."

"They don't aim to kick the ceiling and break it, do they?"

Well, that was quite true, and I'll admit that we went away very anxious. Aggie was inclined to return to the unfortunate incident of the janitor and the furnace pipe when Tish was learning to shoot in the basement some years ago, and to think that she had bought a muffler or whatever it is they put on guns to stop the noise, and was shooting in her flat. I myself inclined toward a boomerang, one of which Tish had seen thrown at a charity matinée, and which had much impressed her. In fact, I happened to know that she had tried it herself at least once, for on entering her sitting room one day unexpectedly my bonnet was cut off my head without the slightest warning. But Hannah had

known about the boomerang, and there would have been no need of secrecy.

However, it was not long before Tish herself explained the mystery, and to do so now I shall return to the previous summer at Lake Penzance. When we arrived in June we found to our dismay that a new golf course had been laid out, and that what was called the tenth hole was immediately behind our cottage. On the very first day of our arrival a golf ball entered the kitchen window and struck Hannah, the maid, just below the breastbone, causing her to sit on the stove. She was three days in bed on her face and had to drink her broth by leaning out over the edge of the bed. This was serious enough, but when gentlemen at different times came to the cottage with parcels wrapped to look like extra shoes, and asked Tish to keep them in the refrigerator on the back porch, we were seriously annoyed. Especially after one of them broke and leaked into the ice-tea pitcher, and Aggie, who is very fond of iced tea, looked cross-eyed for almost half an hour.

Some of the language used, too, was most objectionable, and the innocent children who carried the clubs learned it, for I cannot possibly repeat what a very small urchin said to Tish when she offered him a quarter if he would learn the Shorter Catechism. And even our clergyman's wife — the Ostermaiers have a summer cottage near us — showed what we had observed was the moral deterioration caused by the game. For instance, one day she knocked a ball directly into our garbage can, which happened to have its lid off. Owing to the vines she could not see us, and she hunted for some time, tearing at Aggie's cannas as though they were not there, and finally found her ball in the can.

"Do I pick it out or play it out, caddie?" she called.

"Cost you a shot to pick it out," said the caddie.

"I'll play it," she said. "Give me a spoon."

Well, it appeared that she did not mean a tablespoon, although that was certainly what she needed, for he gave her a club, and she began to dig after the ball. She made eleven jabs at it, and then the can overturned.

"Oh, damn!" she said, and just then Aggie sneezed.

"Darn!" said Mrs. Ostermaier, trying to pretend that that was what she had said before. "Are you there, Miss Carberry?"

"I am," Tish replied grimly.

"I suppose you never expected to see me doing this!"

"Well," Tish said slowly, "if anyone had told me that I would find my clergyman's wife in my garbage can I might have been surprised. Hannah, bring Mrs. Ostermaier the coal shovel."

Looking back I perceive that our dear Tish's obsession dated from that incident, for when Mrs. Ostermaier had cleaned up and moved angrily away she left the old ball, covered with coffee grounds, on the path. I am inclined, too, to think that Tish made a few tentative attempts with the ball almost immediately, for I found my umbrella badly bent that night, and that something had cracked a cane left by Charlie Sands, which Aggie was in the habit of using as a pole when fishing from the dock. Strangely enough, however, her bitterness against the game seemed to grow, rather than decrease.

For instance, one day when Aggie was sitting on the edge of our little dock, fishing and reflecting, and Tish was out in the motorboat, she happened to see a caddie on the roof looking for a ball which had lodged there. She began at once to shout at him to get down and go away, and in her indignation forgot to slow down the engine. The boat therefore went directly through the dock and carried it away, including that portion on which

48

Aggie was sitting. Fortunately Aggie always sat on an air cushion at such times, and as she landed in a sitting position she was able to remain balanced until Tish could turn the boat around and come to the rescue. But the combination of the jar and of opening her mouth to yell unfortunately lost Aggie her upper set, as I have before mentioned.

But it was not long before dear Tish's argus eye had discovered a tragedy on the links. A very pretty girl played steadily, and always at such times a young man would skulk along, taking advantage of trees et cetera to keep out of her sight, while at the same time watching her hungrily. Now and then he varied his method by sitting on the shore of the lake. He would watch her until she came close, and then turn his head and look out over the water. And if ever I saw misery in a human face it was there.

Aggie's heart ached over him, and she carried him a cup of tea one afternoon. He seemed rather surprised, but took it, and Aggie said there was a sweetheart floating in it for him.

"A mermaid, eh?" he said. "Well, I'm for her then. Mermaids haven't any legs, and hence can't play golf, I take it." But he looked out over the lake again and resumed his bitter expression. "You can't tell, though. They may have a water variety, like polo." He sighed and drank the tea absently, but after that he cheered somewhat and finally he asked Aggie a question.

"I wish you'd look at me," he said. "I want an outside opinion. Do I look like a golf hazard?"

"A what?" said Aggie.

"Would you think the sight of me would cut ten yards off a drive, or a foot off a putt?" he demanded.

"You look very nice, I'm sure," Aggie replied. But he only got up and shook the sand off himself and stared after the girl.

"That's it," he said. "Very nice! You've hit it." Then he turned on her savagely, to her great surprise. "If I weren't so blamed nice I'd set off a dozen sticks of dynamite on this crazy links and blow myself up with the last one."

Aggie thought he was a little mad.

We saw him frequently after that, never with the girl, but he began to play the game himself. He took some lessons, too, but Tish had to protest for the way he and the professional talked to each other. Mr. McNab would show him how to fix his feet and even arrange his fingers on the club handle. Then he would drive, and the ball would roll a few feet and stop.

"Well, I suppose I waggled my ear that time, or something," he would say.

"Keep your eye on the ball!" Mr. McNab would yell, dancing about. "Ye've got no strength of character, mon."

"Let me kick it, then. I'll send it farther."

After that they would quarrel, and Tish would have to close the windows.

But Tish's interest in golf was still purely that of the onlooker. This is shown by the fact that at this time and following the incident of the dock she decided that we must all learn to swim. That this very decision was to involve us in the fate of the young man, whose name was Bobby Anderson, could not have been foreseen, or that that involvement would land us in various difficulties and a police station.

Tish approached the swimming matter in her usual convincing way.

"Man," she said, "has conquered all the elements — earth, air, and water. He walks.

He flies. He swims — or should. The normal human being today should be as much at home in water as in the air, and vice versa, to follow the great purpose."

"If that's the great purpose we would have both wings and fins," said Aggie rather truculently, for she saw what was coming. But Tish ignored her.

"Water," she went on, "is sustaining. Hence boats. It is as easy to float the human body as a ship."

"Is it?" Aggie demanded. "I didn't float so you could notice it the night you backed the car into the lake."

"You didn't try," Tish said sternly. "You opened your mouth to yell, and that was the equivalent of a leak in a ship. I didn't say a leaking boat would float, did I?"

We thought that might end it, but it did not. When we went upstairs to bed we heard her filling the tub, and shortly after that she called us into the bathroom. She was lying extended in the tub, with a Turkish towel covering her, and she showed us how, by holding her breath, she simply had to stay on top of the water.

"I advise you both," she said, "to make this experiment tonight. It will give you confidence tomorrow."

We went out and closed the door, and Aggie clutched me by the arm.

"I'll die first, Lizzie," she said. "I don't intend to learn to swim, and I won't. A fortune-teller told me to beware of water, and that lake's full of tin cans."

"She was floating in the tub, Aggie," I said to comfort her, although I felt a certain uneasiness myself.

"Then that's where I'll do my swimming," Aggie retorted, and retired to her room.

The small incident of the next day would not belong in this narrative were it not that

51

it introduced us to a better acquaintance with the Anderson boy, and so led to what follows. For let Charlie Sands say what he will, and he was very unpleasant, the truth remains that our dear Tish's motives were of the highest and purest, and what we attempted was to save the happiness of two young lives.

Be that as it may, on the following morning Tish came to breakfast in a mackintosh and bedroom slippers, with an old knitted sweater and the bloomers belonging to her camping outfit beneath. She insisted after the meal that we similarly attire ourselves, and sat on the veranda while we did so, reading a book on the art of swimming, which she had had for some time.

Although she was her usual calm and forceful self both Aggie and I were very nervous, and for fear of the chill Aggie took a small quantity of blackberry cordial. She felt better after that and would have jumped off the end of the dock, but Tish restrained her, advising her to wet her wrists first and thus to regulate and not shock the pulse.

Tish waded out, majestically indifferent, and we trailed after her. Of what followed I am not quite sure. I know, when we were out to our necks, and either I had stepped on a broken bottle or something had bitten me, she turned and said:

"This will do. I am going to float, Lizzie. Give me time to come to the surface."

She then took a long breath and threw herself back into the water, disappearing at once. I waited for some time, but only a foot emerged, and that only for a second. I might have grown anxious, but it happened that just then Aggie yelled that there was a leech on her, sucking her blood, and I turned to offer her assistance. One way and another it was some time before I turned to look again at Tish — and she had not come up. The water was in a state of turmoil, however, and now and then a hand or a leg emerged.

I was uncertain what to do. Tish does not like to have her plans disarranged, and she had certainly requested me to give her time. I could not be certain, moreover, how much time would be required. While I was debating the matter I was astonished to hear a violent splashing near at hand, and to see Mr. Anderson, fully dressed, approaching us. He said nothing, but waited until Tish's foot again reappeared, and then caught it, thus bringing her to the surface.

For some time she merely stood with her mouth open and her eyes closed. But at last she was able to breathe and to speak, and in spite of my affection for her I still resent the fact that her first words were in anger.

"Lizzie, you are a fool!" she said.

"You said to give you time, Tish."

"Well, you did!" she snapped. "Time to drown." She then turned to Mr. Anderson and said, "Take me in, please. And go slowly. I think I've swallowed a fish."

I got her into the cottage and to bed, and for an hour or two she maintained that she had swallowed a fish and could feel it flopping about inside her. But after a time the sensation ceased and she said that either she had been mistaken or it had died. She was very cold to me.

Mr. Anderson called that afternoon to inquire for her, and we took him to her room. But at first he said very little, and continually consulted his watch and then glanced out the window toward the links. Finally he put the watch away and drew a long breath.

"Four-seven," he said despondently. "Just on time, like a train! You can't beat it."

"What is on time?" Tish asked.

"It's a personal matter," he observed, and lapsed into a gloomy silence.

Aggie went to the window, and I followed. The pretty girl had sent her ball neatly onto the green and, trotting over after it, proceeded briskly to give it a knock and drop it into the cup. He looked up at us with hopeless eyes.

"Holed in one, I suppose?" he inquired.

"She only knocked it once and it went in," Aggie said.

"It would." His voice was very bitter. "She's the champion of this part of the country. She's got fourteen silver cups, two salad bowls, a card tray, and a soup tureen, all trophies. She's never been known to slice, pull, or foozle. When she gets her eye on the ball it's there for keeps. Outside of that, she's a nice girl."

"Why don't you learn the game yourself?" Tish demanded.

"Because I can't. I've tried. You must have heard me trying. I can't even caddie for her. I look at her and lose the ball, and it has got to a stage now where the mere sight of me on the links costs her a stroke a hole. I'll be frank with you," he added after a slight pause. "I'm in love with her. Outside of golf hours she likes me too. But the damned game — sorry, I apologize — the miserable game is separating us. If she'd break her arm or something," he finished savagely, "I'd have a chance."

There was a thoughtful gleam in Tish's eye when he fell into gloomy silence.

"Isn't there any remedy?" she asked.

"Not while she's champion. A good beating would help, but who's to beat her?"

"You can't?"

"Listen," he said. "In the last few months, here and at home, I've had ninety golf lessons, have driven three thousand six hundred balls, of which I lost four hundred and ninety-six, have broken three drivers, one niblick, and one putter. I ask you," he con-

55

cluded drearily, "did you ever hear before of anyone breaking a putter?"

The thoughtful look was still in Tish's eye when he left, but she said nothing. A day or two after, we watched him with Mr. McNab, and although he was standing with his back to the house when he drove, we heard a crash overhead and the sheet-iron affair which makes the stove draw was knocked from the chimney and fell to the ground.

He saw us and waved a hand at the wreckage.

"Sorry," he called. "I keep a roofer now for these small emergencies and I'll send him over." Then he looked at Mr. McNab, who had sat down on a bunker and had buried his face in his hands.

"Come now, McNab," he said. "Cheer up; I've thought of a way. If I'm going to drive behind me, all I have to do is to play the game backwards."

Mr. McNab said nothing. He got up, gave him a furious glance, and then with his hands behind him and his head bent went back toward the clubhouse. Mr. Anderson watched him go, teed another ball, and made a terrific lunge at it. It rose, curved, and went into the lake.

"Last ball!" he called to us cheerfully. "Got one to lend me?"

I sincerely hope I am not doing Tish an injustice, but she certainly said we had not. Yet Mrs. Ostermaier's ball — But she may have lost it. I do not know.

It was Aggie who introduced us to Nettie Lynn, the girl in the case. Aggie is possibly quicker than the rest of us to understand the feminine side of a love affair, for Aggie was at one time engaged to a Mr. Wiggins, a gentleman who had pursued his calling as master roofer on and finally off a roof. (More than once that summer Tish had observed how useful he would have been to us at that time, as we were constantly having broken

slates, and as the water spout was completely stopped with balls.) And Aggie maintained that Nettie Lynn really cared for Mr. Anderson.

"If Mr. Wiggins were living," she said gently, "and if I played golf, if he appeared unexpectedly while I was knocking the ball or whatever it is they do to it, if I really cared — and you know, Tish, I did — I am sure I should play very badly."

"You don't need all those ifs to reach that conclusion," Tish said coldly.

A day or two later Aggie stopped Miss Lynn and offered her some orangeade, and she turned out to be very pleasant and friendly. But when Tish had got the conversation switched to Mr. Anderson she was cool and somewhat scornful.

"Bobby?" she said, lifting her eyebrows. "Isn't he screamingly funny on the links!"

"He's a very fine young man," Tish observed, eying her steadily.

"He has no temperament."

"He has a good disposition. That's something."

"Oh, yes," she admitted carelessly. "He's as gentle as a lamb."

Tish talked it over after she had gone. She said that the girl was all right, but that conceit over her game had ruined her, and that the only cure was for Bobby to learn and then beat her to death in a tournament or something, but that Bobby evidently couldn't learn, and so that was that. She then fell into one of those deep silences during which her splendid mind covers enormous ranges of thought, and ended by saying something to the effect that if one could use a broom one should be able to do something else.

We closed up the cottage soon after and returned to town.

Now and then we saw Nettie Lynn on the street, and once Tish asked us to dinner and we found Bobby Anderson there. He said he had discovered a place in a department

57

store to practice during the winter, with a net to catch the balls, but that owing to his unfortunate tendencies he had driven a ball into the well of the store, where it had descended four stories and hit a manager on the back. He was bent over bowing to a customer or it would have struck his head and killed him.

"She was there," he said despondently. "She used to think I was only a plain fool. Now she says I'm dangerous, and that I ought to take out a license for carrying weapons before I pick up a club."

"I don't know why you want to marry her," Tish said in a sharp voice.

"I don't either," he agreed. "But I do. That's the hell — I beg your pardon — that's the deuce of it."

It was following this meeting that the mysterious events occurred with which I commenced this narrative. And though there may be no connection it was only a day or two later that I read aloud to Aggie an item in a newspaper stating that an elderly woman who refused to give her name had sent a golf ball through the practice net in a downtown store and that the ball had broken and sent off a fire alarm, with the result that the sprinkling system, which was a new type and not dependent on heat, had been turned on in three departments. I do know, however, that Tish's new velvet hat was never seen from that time on, and that on our shopping excursions she never entered that particular store.

In coming now to the events which led up to the reason for Nettie Lynn cutting us, and to Charlie Sands' commentary that his wonderful aunt, Letitia Carberry, should remember the commandment which says that honesty is the best policy — I am sure he was joking, for that is not one of the great Commandments — I feel that a certain explanation is due. This explanation is not an apology for dear Tish, but a statement of her point of view.

Letitia Carberry has a certain magnificence of comprehension. If in this magnificence she loses sight of small things, if she occasionally uses perhaps unworthy methods to a worthy end, it is because to her they are not important. It is only the end that counts.

She has, too, a certain secrecy. But that is because of a nobility which says in effect that by planning alone she assumes sole responsibility. I think also that she has little confidence in Aggie and myself, finding us but weak vessels into which she pours in due time the overflow from her own exuberant vitality and intelligence.

With this in mind I shall now relate the small events of the winter. They were merely straws, showing the direction of the wind of Tish's mind. And I dare say we were not observant. For instance, we reached Tish's apartment one afternoon to find the janitor there in a very ugly frame of mind. "You threw something out of this window, Miss Carberry," he said, "and don't be after denying it."

"What did I throw out of the window?" Tish demanded loftily. "Produce it."

"If it wasn't that it bounced and went over the fence," he said, "I'd be saying it was a flatiron. That parrot just squawked once and turned over."

"Good riddance, too," Tish observed. "The other tenants ought to send me a vote of thanks."

"Six milk bottles on Number Three's fire escape," the janitor went on, counting his fingers; "the wash line broke for Number One and all the clothes dirty, and old Mr. Ferguson leaning out to spit and almost killed — it's no vote of thanks you'll be getting."

When she had got rid of him Tish was her usual cool and dignified self. She offered no explanation and we asked for none. And for a month or so nothing happened. Tish distributed her usual list of improving books at the Sunday-school Christmas treat, and we packed our customary baskets for the poor. On Christmas Eve we sang our usual carols before the homes of our friends, and except for one mischance, owing to not knowing that the Pages had rented their house, all was symbolic of the peace and good will of the festive period. At the Pages', however, a very unpleasant person asked us for ——— sake to go away and let him sleep.

But shortly after the holidays Tish made a proposition to us, and stated that it was a portion of a plan to bring about the happiness of two young and unhappy people.

"In developing this plan," she said, "it is essential that we all be in the best of physical condition; what I believe is known technically as in the pink. You two, for instance, must be able to walk for considerable distances, carrying a weight of some size."

"What do you mean by 'in the pink'?" Aggie asked suspiciously.

"What you are not," Tish said with a certain scorn. "How many muscles have you got?"

"All I need," said Aggie rather acidly.

"And of all you have, can you use one muscle, outside of the ordinary ones that carry you about?"

"I don't need to."

"Have you ever stood up, naked to the air, and felt shame at your flaccid muscles and your puny strength?"

"Really, Tish!" I protested. "I'll walk if you insist. But I don't have to take off my clothes and feel shame at my flabbiness to do it."

She softened at that, and it ended by our agreeing to fall in with her mysterious plan by going to a physical trainer. I confess to a certain tremor when we went for our first

61

induction into the profundities of bodily development. There was a sign outside, with a large picture of a gentleman with enormous shoulders and a pigeon breast, and beneath it were the words: "I will make you a better man." But Tish was confident and calm.

The first day, however, was indeed trying. We found, for instance, that we were expected to take off all our clothing and to put on one-piece jersey garments, without skirts or sleeves, and reaching only to the knees. As if this were not enough, the woman attendant said when we were ready, "In you go, dearies," and shoved us into a large bare room where a man was standing with his chest thrown out, and wearing only a pair of trousers and a shirt which had shrunk to almost nothing. Aggie clutched me by the arm.

"I've got to have stockings, Lizzie!" she whispered. "I don't feel decent."

But the woman had closed the door, and Tish was explaining that we wished full and general muscular development.

"The human body," she said, "instantly responds to care and guidance, and what we wish is simply to acquire perfect coordination. 'The easy slip of muscles underneath the polished skin,' as some poet has put it."

"Yeah," said the man. "All right. Lie down in a row on the mat, and when I count, raise the right leg in the air and drop it. Keep on doing it. I'll tell you when to stop."

"Lizzie!" Aggie threw at me in an agony. "Lizzie, I simply can't!"

"Quick," said the trainer. "I've got four pounds to take off a welterweight this afternoon. Right leg, ladies. Up, down; one, two — "

Never since the time in Canada when Aggie and I were taking a bath in the lake, and a fisherman came and fished from a boat for two hours while we sat in the icy water to our necks, have I suffered such misery.

R I N E H A R T

"Other leg," said the trainer. And later: "Right leg up, cross, up, down. Left leg up, cross, up, down." Aside from the lack of dignity of the performance came very soon the excruciating ache of our weary flesh. Limb by limb and muscle by muscle he made us work, and when we were completely exhausted on the mat he stood us up on our feet in a row and looked us over.

"You've got a long way to go, ladies," he said sternly. "It's a gosh-awful shame the way you women neglect your bodies. Hold in the abdomen and throw out the chest. Balance easily on the ball of the foot. Now touch the floor with the fingertips, as I do."

"Young man," I protested, "I haven't been able to do that since I was sixteen."

"Well, you've had a long rest," he said coldly. "Put your feet apart. That'll help."

When the lesson was over we staggered out, and Aggie leaned against a wall and moaned. "It's too much, Tish," she said feebly. "I'm all right with my clothes on, and anyhow, I'm satisfied as I am. I'm the one to please, not that wretch in there."

Tish, however, had got her breath and said that she felt like a new woman, and that blood had got to parts of her it had never reached before. But Aggie went sound asleep in the cabinet bath and had to be assisted to the cold shower. I mention this tendency of hers to sleep, as it caused us some trouble later on.

In the meantime Tish was keeping in touch with the two young people. She asked Nettie Lynn to dinner one night, and seemed greatly interested in her golf methods. One thing that seemed particularly to interest her was Miss Lynn's device for keeping her head down and her eye on the ball.

"After I have driven," she said, "I make it a rule to count five before looking up."

"How do you see where the ball has gone?" Tish asked.

63

"That is the caddie's business."

"I see," Tish observed thoughtfully, and proceeded for some moments to make pills of her bread and knock them with her fork, holding her head down as she did so.

Another thing which she found absorbing was Miss Lynn's statement that a sound or movement while she drove was fatal, and that even a shadow thrown on the ball while putting decreased her accuracy.

By the end of February we had become accustomed to the exercises and now went through them with a certain sprightliness, turning back somersaults with ease, and I myself now being able to place my flat hand on the floor while standing. Owing to the cabinet baths I had lost considerable flesh and my skin seemed a trifle large for me in places, while Aggie looked, as dear Tish said, like a picked sparerib.

At the end of February, however, our training came to an abrupt end, owing to a certain absent-mindedness on Tish's part. Tish and Aggie had gone to the gymnasium without me, and at ten o'clock that night I telephoned Tish to ask if Aggie was spending the night with her. To my surprise Tish said nothing for a moment, and then asked me in a strained voice to put on my things at once and meet her at the door to the gymnasium building.

Quick as I was, she was there before me, hammering at the door of the building, which appeared dark and deserted. It appeared that the woman had gone home early with a cold, and that Tish had agreed to unfasten the bath cabinet and let Aggie out at a certain time, but that she had remembered leaving the electric iron turned on at home and had hurried away, leaving Aggie asleep and helpless in the cabinet.

The thought of our dear Aggie, perspiring her life away, made us desperate, and on

finding no response from within the building Tish led the way to an alleyway at the side and was able to reach the fire escape. With mixed emotions I watched her valiant figure disappear, and then returned to the main entrance, through which I expected her to reappear with our unhappy friend.

But we were again unfortunate. A few moments later the door indeed was opened, but to give exit to Tish in the grasp of a very rude and violent watchman, who immediately blew loudly on a whistle. I saw at once that Tish meant to give no explanation which would involve taking a strange man into the cabinet room, where our hapless Aggie was completely disrobed and helpless; and to add to our difficulties three policemen came running and immediately placed us under arrest.

Fortunately the station house was near, and we were saved the ignominy of a police wagon. Tish at once asked permission to telephone Charlie Sands, and as he is the night editor of a newspaper he was able to come at once. But Tish was of course reticent as to her errand before so many men, and he grew slightly impatient.

"All right," he said. "I know you were in the building. I know how you got in. But why? I don't think you were after lead pipe or boxing gloves, but these men do."

"I left something there, Charlie."

"Go a little further. What did you leave there?"

"I can't tell you. But I've got to go back there at once. Every moment now — "

"Get this," said Charlie Sands sternly: "Either you come over with the story or you'll be locked up. And I'm bound to say I think you ought to be."

In the end Tish told the unhappy facts, and two reporters, the sergeant and the policemen were all deeply moved. Several got out their handkerchiefs, and the sergeant turned

quite red in the face. One and all they insisted on helping to release our poor Aggie, and most of them escorted us back to the building, only remaining in the corridor at our request while we entered the cabinet room.

Although we had expected to find Aggie in a parboiled condition the first thing which greeted us was a violent sneeze.

"Aggie!" I called desperately.

She sneezed again, and then said in a faint voice, "Hurry up. I'b dearly frozed."

We learned later that the man in charge had turned off all the electricity when he left, from a switch outside, and that Aggie had perspired copiously and been on the verge of apoplexy until six o'clock, and had nearly frozen to death afterwards. Tish draped a sheet around the cabinet, and the policemen et cetera came in. Aggie gave a scream when she saw them, but it was proper enough, with only her head showing, and they went out at once to let her get her clothing on.

Before he put us in a taxicab that night Charlie Sands spoke to Tish with unjustifiable bitterness.

"I have given the watchman twenty dollars for that tooth you loosened, Aunt Tish," he said. "And I've got to set up some food for the rest of this outfit. Say, fifty dollars, for which you'd better send me a check." He then slammed the door, but opened it immediately. "I just want to add this," he said: "If my revered grandfather has turned over in his grave as much as I think he has, he must be one of the liveliest corpses underground."

I am happy to record that Aggie suffered nothing more than a heavy cold in the head. But she called Tish up the next morning and with unwonted asperity said, " I do thig, Tish, that you bight have put a strig aroud your figer or sobethig, to rebeber be by!"

It was but a week or two after this that Tish called me up and asked me to go to her apartment quickly, and to bring some arnica from the drugstore. I went as quickly as possible, to find Hannah on the couch in the sitting room moaning loudly, and Tish putting hot flannels on her kneecap.

"It's broken, Miss Tish," she groaned. "I know it is."

"Nonsense," said Tish. "Anyhow I called to you to stay out."

In the center of the room was a queer sort of machine, with a pole on an iron base and a dial at the top, and a ball fastened to a wire. There was a golf club on the floor.

Later on, when Hannah had been helped to her room and an arnica compress adjusted, Tish took me back and pointed to the machine.

"Two hundred and twenty yards, Lizzie," she said, "and would have registered more but for Hannah's leg. That's driving."

She then sat down and told me the entire plan. She had been working all winter, and was now confident that she could defeat Nettie Lynn. She had, after her first experience in the department store, limited herself — in another store — to approach shots. For driving she had used the machine. For putting she had cut a round hole in the carpet and had sawed an opening in the floor beneath, in which she had placed a wide-mouthed jar.

"My worst trouble, Lizzie," she said, "was lifting my head. But I have solved it. See here."

She then produced a short leather strap, one end of which she fastened to her belt and the other she held in her teeth. She had almost lost a front tooth at the beginning, she said, but that phase was over.

"I don't even need it anymore," she told me. "Tomorrow I shall commence placing an

egg on the back of my neck as I stoop, and that with a feeling of perfect security."

She then looked at me with her serene and confident glance.

"It has been hard work, Lizzie," she said. "It is not over. It is even possible that I may call on you to do things which your ethical sense will at first reject. But remember this, and then decide: The happiness of two young and tender hearts is at stake."

She seemed glad of a confidante, and asked me to keep a record of some six practice shots, as shown by the dial on the machine. I have this paper before me as I write:

1st drive, 230 yards. Slight pull.

2nd drive, 245 yards. Direct.

3rd drive, 300 yards. Slice.

4th drive, 310 yards. Direct.

5th drive. Wire broke.

6th drive. Wire broke again. Ball went through windowpane. Probably hit dog, as considerable howling outside.

She then showed me her clubs, of which she had some forty-six, not all of which, however, she approved of. It was at that time that dear Tish taught me the names of some of them, such as niblick, stymie, cleek, mashie, putter, stance, and brassie, and observed mysteriously that I would need my knowledge later on. She also advised that before going back to Penzance we walk increasing distances every day.

"Because," she said, "I shall need my two devoted friends this summer; need them perhaps as never before."

I am bound to confess, however, that on our return to Penzance Tish's first outdoor work at golf was a disappointment. She had a small ritual when getting ready; thus she

69

would say, firmly, suiting the action to the phrase: "Tee ball. Feet in line with ball, advance right foot six inches, place club, overlap right thumb over left thumb, drop arms, left wrist rigid, head down, eye on the ball, shoulders steady, body still. Drive!" Having driven she then stood and counted five slowly before looking up.

At first, however, she did not hit the ball, or would send it only a short distance. But she worked all day, every day, and we soon saw a great improvement. As she had prophesied, she used us a great deal. For instance, to steady her nerves she would have us speak to her when driving, and even fire a revolver out toward the lake.

We were obliged to stop this, however, for we were in the habit of using the barrel buoy of the people next door to shoot at, until we learned that it was really not a buoy at all, but some fine old whiskey which they were thus concealing, and which leaked out through the bullet holes.

We were glad to find that Nettie Lynn and Bobby were better friends than they had been the year before, and to see his relief when Tish told him to give up his attempts at golf altogether.

"I shall defeat her so ignominiously, Bobby," she said, "that she will never wish to hear of the game again."

"You're a great woman, Miss Carberry," he said solemnly.

"But you, too, must do your part."

"Sure I'll do my part. Name it to me, and that is all."

But he looked grave when she told him.

"First of all," she said, "you are to quarrel with her the night before the finals. Violently."

"Oh, I say!"

"Second, when she is crushed with defeat you are to extract a promise, an oath if you like, that she is through with golf."

"You don't know her," he said. "Might as well expect her to be through with her right hand."

But he agreed to think it over and, going out to the lakefront, sat for a long time lost in thought. When he came back he agreed, but despondently.

"She may love me after all this," he said, "but I'm darned if I think she'll like me."

But he cheered up later and planned the things they could do when they were both free of golf and had some time to themselves. And Mr. McNab going by at that moment, he made a most disrespectful gesture at his back.

It is painful, in view of what followed, to recall his happiness at that time.

I must confess that Aggie and I were still in the dark as to our part in the tournament. And our confusion as time went on was increased by Tish's attitude toward her caddie. On her first attempt he had been impertinent enough, goodness knows, and Tish had been obliged to reprove him.

"Your business here, young man," she said, "is to keep your eye on the ball."

"That's just what you're not doing," he said smartly. "Lemme show you."

Tish said afterwards that it was purely an accident, for he broke every rule of stance and so on, but before she realized his intention he had taken the club from her hand and sent the ball entirely out of sight.

"That's the way," he said. "Whale 'em!"

But recently her attitude to him had changed. She would bring him in and give him

cake and ginger ale, and she paid him far too much. When Hannah showed her disapproval he made faces at her behind Tish's back, and once he actually put his thumb to his nose. To every remonstrance Tish made but one reply.

"Develop the larger viewpoint," she would observe, "and remember this: I do nothing without a purpose."

"Then stop him making snoots at me," said Hannah. "I'll poison him, that's what I'll do."

Thus our days went on. The hours of light Tish spent on the links. In the evenings her busy fingers were not idle, for she was making herself some knickerbockers from an old pair of trousers which Charlie Sands had left at the cottage, cutting them off below the knee and inserting elastic in the hem, while Aggie and I, by the shade of our lamp, knitted each a long woolen stocking to complete the outfit.

It was on such an evening that Tish finally revealed her plan, that plan which has caused so much unfavorable comment since. The best answer to that criticism is Tish's own statement to us that night.

"Frankly," she admitted, "the girl can beat me. But if she does she will continue on her headstrong way, strewing unhappiness hither and yon. She must not win!"

Briefly the plan she outlined was based on the undermining of Nettie's morale. Thus, Aggie sneezes during the hay-fever season at the mere sight of a sunflower. She was to keep one in her pocket, and at a signal from Tish was to sniff at it, holding back the resultant sneeze, however, until the champion was about to drive.

"I'll be thirty yards behind, with the crowd, won't I?" Aggie asked.

"You will be beside her," Tish replied solemnly. "On the day of the finals the caddies

73

will go on a strike, and I shall insist that a strange caddie will spoil my game, and ask for you."

It appeared that I was to do nothing save to engage Mr. McNab in conversation at certain times and thus distract his attention, the signal for this being Tish placing her right hand in her trousers pocket. For a sneeze from Aggie the signal was Tish coughing once.

"At all times, Aggie," she finished, "I shall expect you to keep ahead of us, and as near Nettie Lynn's ball as possible. The undulating nature of the ground is in our favor, and will make it possible now and then for you to move it into a less favorable position. If at the fourteenth hole you can kick it into the creek it will be very helpful."

Aggie was then rehearsed in the signals, and did very well indeed.

Mr. McNab was an occasional visitor those days. He was watching Tish's game with interest.

"Ye'll never beat the champion, ma'm," he would say, "but ye take the game o' gowf as it should be taken, wi' humility and prayer."

More than once he referred to Bobby Anderson, saying that he was the only complete failure of his experience, and that given a proper chance he would make a golfer of him yet.

"The mon has aye the build of a gowfer," he would say wistfully.

It is tragic now to remember that incident of the day before the opening of the tournament, when Bobby came to our cottage and we all ceremoniously proceeded to the end of the dock and flung his various clubs, shoes, balls, cap, and bag into the lake, and then ate a picnic supper on the shore. When the moon came up he talked of the future in glowing terms.

"I feel in my bones, Miss Tish," he said, "that you will beat her. And I know her; she won't stand being defeated, especially by — " Here he coughed, and lost the thread of this thought. "I'm going to buy her a horse," he went on. "I'm very fond of riding."

He said, however, that it was going to be very hard for him to quarrel with her the evening before the finals.

"I'm too much in love," he confessed. "Besides, outside of golf we agree on everything — politics, religion, bridge; everything."

It was then that Tish made one of her deeply understanding comments.

"Married life is going to be very dull for you both," she said.

It was arranged that in spite of the quarrel he should volunteer to caddie for the champion the day of the strike, and to take a portion of Aggie's responsibility as to changing the lie of the ball, and so forth. He was not hopeful, however.

"She won't want me any more than the measles," he said.

"She can't very well refuse, before the crowd," Tish replied.

I pass with brief comment over the early days of the women's tournament. Mrs. Ostermaier was eliminated the first day with a score of 208, and slapped her caddie on the seventeenth green. Tish turned in only a fair score, and was rather depressed; so much so that she walked in her sleep and wakened Aggie by trying to tee a ball on the end of her — Aggie's — nose. But the next day she was calm enough, and kept her nerves steady by the simple device of knitting as she followed the ball. The result was what she had expected, and the day of the finals saw only Nettie Lynn and our dear Tish remaining.

All worked out as had been expected. The caddies went on a strike that day, and before the field Nettie was obliged to accept Bobby's offer to carry her clubs. But he was very gloomy and he brought his troubles to me.

"Well, I've done it," he said. "And I'm ruined for life. She never wants to see me again. It's my belief," he added gloomily, "that she could have bit the head off an iron club last night and never have known she had done it."

He groaned and mopped his face with his handkerchief.

"I'm not sure it's the right thing after all," he said. "The madder she is the better she'll play. All she's got to do is to imagine I'm the ball, and she'll knock it a thousand yards."

There was some truth in this probably, for she certainly overshot the first hole, and the way she said "Mashie!" to Bobby Anderson really sounded like an expletive. Tish won that hole, they halved the second, and owing to Aggie sneezing without apparent cause during Tish's drive on the third, Nettie took it. On the fourth, however, Tish was fortunate and drove directly into the cup.

We now entered the undulating portion of the course, and I understand that Bobby and Aggie both took advantage of this fact to place Nettie Lynn's ball in occasional sand traps, and once to lose it altogether. Also that the device of sneezing during a putt was highly effective, so that at the ninth hole dear Tish was three up.

Considering the obloquy which has fallen to me for my own failure to cooperate, I can only state as follows: I engaged Mr. McNab steadily in conversation, and when he moved to a different position I faithfully followed him; but I was quite helpless when he suddenly departed, taking an oblique course across the field, nor could I approach Tish to warn her.

And on the surface all continued to go well. It was now evident to all that the champion was defeated, and that the champion knew it herself. In fact the situation was hopeless, and no one, I think, was greatly surprised when after driving for the fourteenth hole she suddenly threw down her club, got out her handkerchief and left the course, followed by Bobby.

Our misfortune was that Aggie was ahead in the hollow and did not see what had happened. Her own statement is that she saw the ball come and fall into a dirt road, and that all she did was to follow it and step on it, thus burying it out of sight; but also that no sooner had she done this than Mr. McNab came charging out of the woods like a mad bull and rushed at her, catching her by the arm.

It was at that moment that our valiant Tish, flushed with victory, came down the slope.

Mr. McNab was dancing about and talking in broad Scotch, but Tish finally caught the drift of what he was saying — that he had suspected us all day, that we would go before the club board, and that Tish would get no cup.

"You've played your last gowf on these links, Miss Carberry, and it's a crying shame the bad name you've gien us," was the way he finished, all the time holding to Aggie's arm. It was thus I found them.

"Very well," Tish said in her coldest tone. "I shall be very glad to state before the board my reasons, which are excellent. Also to register a protest against using the lakefront before my cottage for the cooling of beer, et cetera. I dare say I may go home first?"

"I'll be going with you, then."

"Very well," Tish replied. "And be good enough to release Miss Pilkington. She was

merely obeying my instructions." Thus our lionhearted Tish, always ready to assume responsibility, never weakening, always herself.

I come now to a painful portion of this narrative, and the reason for Nettie Lynn cutting us dead on the street. For things moved rapidly within the next few moments. Mr. McNab settled himself like a watchdog on our cottage steps, and there Tish herself carried him some blackberry cordial and a slice of coconut cake. There, too, in her impressive manner she told him the story of the plot.

"Think of it, Mr. McNab," she said. "Two young and loving hearts yearning for each other, and separated only by the failure of one of them to learn the game of golf!"

Mr. McNab was profoundly moved.

"He wouldna keep his eye on the ball," he said huskily. "I like the lad fine, but he would aye lift his heid."

"If this brings them together you would not part them, would you?"

"He wouldna fallow through, Miss Carberry. He juist hit the ball an' quit."

"If they were married, and he could give his mind to the game he'd learn it, Mr. McNab."

The professional brightened. "Maybe. Maybe," he said. "He has the body of the gowfer. If he does that, we'll say na mair, Miss Carberry."

And, do what we would, Mr. McNab stood firm on that point. The thought of his failure with Bobby Anderson had rankled, and now he made it a condition of his silence on the day's events that he have a free hand with him that summer.

"Gie him to me for a month," he said, "and he'll be a gowfer, and na care whether he's married or no."

79

We ate our dinner that night in a depressed silence, although Tish's silver cup graced the center of the table. Before we had finished, Bobby Anderson came bolting in and kissed us each solemnly.

"It's all fixed," he said. "She has solemnly sworn never to play golf again, and I've brought her clubs down to follow mine into the lake."

"You'd better keep them," Tish said. "You're going to need them."

She then broke the news to him, and considering the months she had spent to help him he was very ungrateful, I must say. Indeed, his language was shocking.

"Me learn golf?" he shouted. "You tell McNab to go to perdition and take his cursed golf links with him. I won't do it! This whole scheme was to eliminate golf from my life. It has pursued me for three years. I have nightmares about it. I refuse. Tell McNab I've broken my leg. Wait a minute and I'll go out and break it."

But he could not refuse, and he knew it.

So far as we know, Nettie Lynn has never played golf since. She impresses me as a person of her word. But why she should be so bitter toward us we cannot understand. As dear Tish frequently remarks, who could have foreseen that Mr. McNab would actually make a golfer out of Bobby? Or that he would become so infatuated with the game as to abandon practically everything else?

They are married now, and Hannah knows their cook. She says it is sometimes nine o'clock at night in the summer before he gets in to dinner.

DR. JOHNSON ON THE LINKS

On the morning after our arrival in St. Andrews Dr. Johnson expressed a desire to see the ruins of ecclesiastical antiquity for which this place is famous, or, I should say, infamous. Yielding to a roguish temptation of which I am ashamed, and which even now astonishes me, I determined to practice on the credulity of my venerated friend. I therefore, under pretence of leading Dr. Johnson to the ruins, carried him to that part of the vicinity which is called the Links. It is an undulating stretch of grassy land, varied by certain small elevations, which I assured Dr. Johnson covered all the ecclesiastical ruins that time and the licence of the rabble had spared.

He was much moved, and refused to be covered, as on consecrated ground, while he walked along the Links, a course of some two miles. Often he would pause, and I heard him mutter *perierunt etiam ruinæ*. I ventured to ask him his opinion of John Knox, when he replied, in a sensible agitation, "Sir, he was worthy to be the opprobrious leader of your opprobrious people." I was hardly recovered from this blow at my nation, when Dr. Johnson's wig was suddenly and violently removed from his head, and carried to a certain distance. We were unable to account for this circumstance, and Dr.

ANDREW LANG

Johnson was just about stooping to regain his property, when a rough fellow, armed with a few clubs, of which some had threatening heads of iron, came up hastily, saying, "Hoot awa'! ye maunna stir the hazard." It appears that his golf ball, struck by him from a distance, had displaced Dr. Johnson's wig, and was still reposing in his folds. Before I could interfere the fellow had dealt a violent stroke at the perruque, whence the ball, soaring in an airy curve, alighted at a considerable distance. I have seldom seen my venerable friend more moved than by this unexpected assault upon his dignity. "Sir," said he to the fellow, "you have taken an unwarranted liberty with one who neither provokes nor pardons insult." At the same moment he hastily disembarrassed himself of his coat, and appeared in shirt-sleeves, which reminded me of his avowed lack of partiality for clean linen. Assuming an attitude of self-defence, he planted one blow on his adversary's nose, and another in his abdomen, with such impetuosity and science that the rascal fell, and bellowed for mercy. This Dr. Johnson was pleased to grant, after breaking all his weapons. He then resumed his coat, and, with an air of good-humored triumph, he remarked, "It is long, sir, since I knocked a man down, and I feel myself the better for the exercise."

At this moment we came within view of the Cathedral towers, and I instantly felt considerable apprehension lest, on discovering my trick, he might bestow on me the same correction as he had just administered to the golfer. I therefore hastily took the opportunity to call his attention to the towers, remarking that they were the remains of certain small chapels, which had suffered less from the frenzy of the rabble than the Cathedral, on whose site, as I told him, we were now walking. Thus I endeavored to give him a higher, and possibly an exaggerated, idea of the ancient resources and ecclesiastical magnificence of my country.

"Sir," he said, "we will examine later the contemptible relics which the idiotic fury of your ancestors has spared; meantime I must have a Roll. It is a long time, sir, since I had a Roll." He then, to my alarm, ascended the highest of certain knolls or hummocks, laid himself down at full length, and permitted himself to revolve slowly over and over till he reached the level ground. He was now determined to exercise himself at the game of Golf, which I explained to him as the Scotch form of cricket. Having purchased a ball and club, he threw himself into the correct attitude, as near as he could imitate it, and delivered a blow with prodigious force. Chancing to strike at the same time both the ball and the ground, the head of his club flew off to an immense distance. He was pleased with this instance of his prowess, but declined, on the score of expense, to attempt another experiment. "Sir," he said, "if Goldsmith were here, he would try to persuade us that he could urge a sphere to a greater distance and elevation than yonder gentleman who has just hit over that remote sand pit." Knowing his desire for information, I told him that, in Scotch, a sand pit is called a Bunker. "Sir," said he, "I wonder out of what *colluvies* of barbarism your people selected the jargon which you are pleased to call a language. Sir, you have battened on the broken meats of human speech, and have carried away the bones. A sand pit, sir, is a sand pit."

I was somewhat deadened by this unlooked-for reception of an innocent remark. Meanwhile he had fallen into an abstracted fit, from which I attempted to rouse him, by asking him what he would do if landed on a desert island, with no company but a Cannibal.

"Sir," he said, "I should consider myself more fortunately situated than when landed on an island, equally uncultivated, with no companion but an inquisitive Scotchman.

84

From a Cannibal, sir, I could learn much. From you I can neither learn anything, nor have I any confidence in my power to communicate to you the elements of civilized behavior."

He burst on this into a hearty fit of laughter, which was concluded by a golf ball, which suddenly flew, from an incredible distance, into his mouth, and produced an alarming fit of coughing. When he had recovered from this paroxysm he appeared somewhat disinclined for further conversation, and, on arriving at our inn, he said, "Sir, do not let us meet again till dinner. Sir, you have brought me to a strange place of singular manners. I did not believe, sir, that in his Majesty's dominions there was any district so barbarous, and so perilous to travelers."

Finding him in this mood, and observing that he grasped his staff in a menacing manner, I withdrew to a neighboring tavern.

C O N T R I B U T O R S

RING LARDNER (1885–1933) established the literary tone — imitated by modern satirists of the genre — for humorously told sports stories. He began his career as a sportswriter, gaining a national audience as his column became syndicated throughout the country. Lardner is best known for *You Know Me, Al* (1916), a wildly witty collection of baseball and boxing stories, and the widely anthologized "Haircut" and "The Golden Honeymoon," both hailed as American classics. "Tee Time" was written in 1929.

STEPHEN LEACOCK (1869–1944), Canada's foremost humorist, essayist, and biographer, was an economist and tenured professor of political science at McGill College in Montreal. In 1912 when Leacock's bestselling satirical novel *Sunshine Sketches of a Little Town* was published, it caused a nationwide scandal. Oftentimes compared to *Main Street* and *Huckleberry Finn* for its shocking candor, the book was a scathing portrait of small–minded, small–town life in the provinces. "Golfomaniac" was written in 1943.

DON MARQUIS (1878–1937), the devilishly irreverent poet and playwright, is certainly best remembered for his satire *Archy and Mehitabel* (1927), the story of a love affair between a cockroach and a cat. Like Damon Runyon, Marquis used his characters' cynical wit to voice his own views on politics and social mores. "The Rivercliff Golf Killings" was written in 1921.

MARY ROBERTS RINEHART (1876–1958), playwright and author of virtually hundreds of mysteries, short stories, and serial fiction, was the highest–paid magazine writer of her day. Rinehart's famous novels *The Circular Staircase* and *The Man in Lower Ten* introduced the clever "Had-I-But-Known" formula, in which a mystery within a mystery must be understood before the greater problem can be solved. "Tish Plays the Game" was written in 1926.

ANDREW LANG (1844–1912) was Scotland's most highly honored and prolific historian, poet, journalist, translator, folklorist, and mystic. He compiled and edited twelve wonderful volumes of children's fairy tales, beginning with *The Blue Fairy Book* (1889) and ending with *The Lilac Fairy Book* (1912). All are widely read and still in print today. Lang wrote the classic *The Princess Nobody: A Tale of Fairyland* (1884), illustrated by his friend, Richard Doyle. It is a valuable edition that collectors of rare children's books hold most dear. "Dr. Johnson on the Links" was written in 1897.